CW01502375

Twenty-four Seven Blossom

JULIA BIRD grew up in Gloucestershire and now lives in London. She works part-time for the Poetry School, and as an independent live literature producer.

ALSO BY JULIA BIRD

Hannah and the Monk (Salt, 2008)

Twenty-four Seven Blossom

by

JULIA BIRD

For lovely Sam
of the back row

Julia xxx

SALT

CROMER

PUBLISHED BY SALT PUBLISHING
12 Norwich Road, Cromer, Norfolk NR27 0AX

Salt Publishing 2013

Printed in the UK by TJ International Ltd, Padstow, Cornwall

Typeset in Paperback 9 / 13

ISBN 978 1 907773 56 3 hardback

1 3 5 7 9 8 6 4 2

for Florence

Contents

Thirty-two Girls   1

Poem to be Read on One Breath: Lilac   2

A Kingfisher   3

Hands Together, Eyes Closed   4

On Visiting a Church Built to the Same Dimensions
     as Noah's Ark   5

A Jar of Jam Is In My Hand   8

Bones   9

This Does Me for Snow   10

All the Dark   12

You Could Be Better Off Than You Are   13

Today's Special   14

Poem To Be Read on One Breath: Red   16

Poppet   17

Like a Monkey Fighting a Lizard, Endlessly   18

Monkey Puzzle   20

Poem To Be Read on One Breath: Gold   21

Script for a Lecture on the English Rabbit
     for a W.I. eg   22

Press Play   24

Welcome to Chinatown   27

Self Portrait with 40 Foot of Banquet Roll   29

THREE POEMS FOR MARGARET FOUNTAINE   31

Party, 1 a.m.   39

Koko the Signing Gorilla Tells Us About Her Day   40

The Boast   42

Poem to be Read on One Breath: Emerald   43

Love Poem, with Artemia nyos   44

As they pulled you out of the oxygen tent /
   you asked for the latest party   45
Parrot Spotter   46
There are Sixty-two Pieces of Lego for
   Every Person on the Planet   47
Poem to be Read on One Breath: Rose   49
If You Do That, I Am Forced To Do This   50
to be shone on his body   51
It's Not The Years, Honey, It's the Mileage   52
Poem in Which God at 1% is Acknowledged   53
Poem to be Read on One Breath: Blue   55
A Pebble Cairn   56
Victoria Street Reel   58
The Preservation of Flowers   59

Notes   61

Acknowledgements

Acknowledgements are due to the editors of the anthologies, magazines, apps and websites where some of these poems first appeared – *Birdbook* (Sidekick Books), *The Emma Press Anthology of Mildly Erotic Verse*, *The Erotic Review*, *Horizon Review*, *Lung Jazz: Young British Poets for Oxfam* (Cinnamon Press), the *Poem In Which* blog, The Poetry Archive, *Rising*, *University of Reading Creative Arts Anthology 2009* and the *Words in Air* app.

Thank you to Bea Colley of Southbank Centre, Chris Gribble of Writers' Centre Norwich, Suzy Joinson of the British Council and Caroline Wiseman of Aldeburgh Lookout for the commissions.

Thank you also to everyone who has inspired and improved these poems during their writing, particularly Roddy and especially Andy.

Twenty-four Seven Blossom

Thirty-two Girls

One wants only to wear her long plaits in a bun,
    one bites down on a coral teething ring.
One sings to her governess, her voice
    an echo breath, one is a governess.
One's house is built on stilts above a river,
    one has, like you, a crooked index finger.
These thirty-two are your four-times-great grandmothers,
    and what they'd say is 'Sit down once among us
and draw for the young ones birds to colour in,
    and share with the others, everything you've known.'

Poem to be Read on One Breath: Lilac

she says she's heard *lip-readers can't distinguish between the word 'comfortable' and the words 'I love you'* so I tell her that my hairdresser who has a lilac lily in an ossuary of blackwork skulls tattooed on his forearm always asks if I'm comfortable with the temperature of the water gurgling about my ears and that one day I will answer *I love you too* over the noise of the dozen driers and last year's Ministry of Sound CD compilation as he dollops on the conditioner

A Kingfisher

One sat, in plain sight, downstream.
The sun, pinning stars to the water.

Feathers the colours of jockey silks. Luck.
Whether that's something I saw for myself

or a page turned down in a bird book or a feature
I watched on tv, I don't know – though

I did once peck a fish clean from a plate
with a flat wooden fork. I have felt a thought

dart from its perch in my best imagination
to flash about the branches of a stranger's brain,

and have brought home from a shop in a blue plastic bag
a half a dozen perfect tangerines.

Hands Together, Eyes Closed

for A & M

Because the music's loud
and the wind and the waves are so loud
we must amplify our conversation,
use finger snaps and pointing thumbs
to underscore our chat with pidgin Sign

and puppetry. Cupped hands, balled fists.
Flashed palms full of nothing but the future.
All we say will show on the wall behind us:
a shadow rabbit made from our six hands.
Sometimes what we pray for, someone grants.

On Visiting a Church Built to the Same Dimensions as Noah's Ark

[1] It's one thing to model secular building stock on the lines of Noah's Ark – cubit for cubit the measurements translate perfectly to aircraft hangars, or boat huts for slightly less than ark-sized super-yachts – but this architect built a church.

[2] He chartered a space with an air of stern and prow, piped parishioners aboard and called them crew.

[3] In such a space, the moment a sermon springs leaks in its logic or hymns spin off to a pitch too high to sing, the great west doors will bang and in they come: lioness and lion, first of the two-by-twos.

[4] Their claws click down the aisle as they make their way to their first class cabin, and while they await the call to the captain's table, in file all the rest, beasts of the earth and the creeping things: zebras, llamas, donkeys, chimps, damp from the drizzle, humming the smell of wet rug.

[5] Hutches and cages are piled six deep against the chancel wall as wild and farm, zoo and pet sort themselves a berth.

[6] Snakes are stacked like freight, black and polar bears are battery-tight.

[7] Here come two albatross, two barnacles, two death watch beetles, boring themselves a home in a load-bearing wooden beam.

[8] Every space is filled.

[9] Even the band on your sailor's hat is taut on

a matchbox of germs that need to stay dry.

¹⁰ Impossible or true, on and on they board.

¹¹ While whales and dolphins bob like tugs in the ark's wake and birds perch on the roof, what do you do about dogs?

¹² Would a couple of street dogs be enough, the sort bred back to basics: knee-high, wily, rough plain coats?

¹³ Or would you also need the fancy ranks, the sugar bags of yap and fluff, plus those whose pedigree's part pit pony, part wolf?

¹⁴ Build the Crufts Deck.

¹⁵ X more dozen double kennels, and slide the last bolt home on silence.

¹⁶ No bark or trumpet.

¹⁷ An unrocked boat for a single second till the first hungry marmoset sniffs the air and a million metabolisms come on watch – grazers, hunters and scavengers who won't last forty minutes without eating.

¹⁸ The quick fix is the food chain laid from the top deck down to steerage: long term this idea won't float, so into the already overloaded ark you pack hay nets, food bowls and salt licks, barrels of rum-soaked orchids for the nectar sippers, and in every spare corner, wedged and bent, bundles of fibrous, splintered, juiceless stalks for the bamboorexic pandas.

¹⁹ This thought's voyage is fully underway.

²⁰ It's too far out to sea to head back to safe

port, press on we must and face the inevitable consequence.

21 Good God, the mess.

22 The crap, the cack, the piss.

23 The cobbled piles of pachyderm manure, owl pellets, bird lime, a slurried flood of cow pats and fly spots rising more quickly than you ever could muck out, already up to the ruffs of the choirboys.

24 Forgive them their panic as they scuttle the ship and let the animals escape in flocks, in packs, in herds.

25 A swarm.

26 Stampede.

27 The minute blueprints for this brick-built ark were laid, holes ripped in the story's hull and the sea came pouring in.

28 It's one thing to think unsinkable but speaking it aloud?

29 No sooner said than sunk, all hands and hooves and trotters lost.

30 This is the ship's log.

31 Every page of it is perforated.

32 One by one we tear them out, fold them into origami boats, take them to the beach and hope they're buoyant when the waters rise.

A Jar of Jam Is In My Hand

How would it be if a jar of jam slipped,
or was let slip, and blew itself to bits
on the shock of a stone-flagged floor?
Golly, such a quality of mess!
Glass – snipped whiskers and needles,
the super goo of jam. Would you try
and sweep it up? Would you try
and scrape? It is fearsome and a thrill
that the world's this full of small chaos,
all possible, paused on the point of release.
To transfer eggs from the hen to the pan
risks the hundred watt splatter of yolk
on the ground. Screw in a bulb a shade
too tight, it smashes in your fist and spills
its light in streams. You hear tell, and often,
of rivers that have burst their banks,
and what's to stop the banks themselves
unleashing cash in minuscule denominations
to silt up streets with cent and penny screes?
Scrabbling up to the top of the copper pile,
atoms and humours all aslosh within me – My,
how permeable I feel today!
A jar of jam is in my hand, its pin is out.

Bones

The dog done in oils to hang in the gun room,
the one with nine shades of pink in the mouth
which never marked a shot bird's skin

and the Scottie dog which modelled and was struck in lead
a million miniature times, each cast taken
on the same short walkies round a square of London

and the dog dressed in a bandana,
framed turning his fleas over in the long shot
concluding the coming-of-age drama,

are long gone, brought to heel by art
not knowing what it meant to be so caught.
The good dog sat now at my feet

is not holding out a paw for you to shake.
He barely remembers yesterday's bone.
He barely imagines tomorrow's bone.

This Does Me for Snow

A bed's made in a hurry.
The blanket settles
and the awkward contours

of a kicked-off sock or a paperback
are soothed, and this
does me for snow,

while these sweet equivalencies
put the pink in my cheeks
and a snap in my bunting:

the whoof of a Tube pulling into the station,
the hand dryer's hot down-draught,
the small mistral from a slammed novel.

Fog where the cold front of an ice cube
meets the ambient heat of the gin;
fog where the juniper and lime roll in

hitting the dewpoint
again and again.
Gauzification of the brain.

Imaginary friends!
Hey, dream lovers and drama queens!
Yesterday, the neighbour's cat seeped into my house

through an open window,
and somewhere today a dog, torrential,
has set in barking for the afternoon.

All the Dark

Someone bought and stockpiled all the dark:
left me merely with this shoddy murk
of browned-out seascapes spoilt by rig-flares
and overflown by Boeings freighting backlit signs
of burning cigarettes. Someone lashes fields
awake with rope-light miles of pre-dawn motorways
and someone cuts clip shows from neon, flash and glare
and plays them even when I've closed my eyes.

Bring me details of the warehouse where
the dark is stored. I'll raid it to reclaim
the depths of midnight mines underneath
a month of glass ring moons. I will own again
dark as backdrop, dark as a blackout
for batteries of astonishing ignitions.

You Could Be Better
Off Than You Are

after 'Light bulb to Simulate Moonlight' by Katie Paterson

Say the moon's a clock that strikes monthly.
We count its chimes – one for every paycheque,
two to book a haircut, nine for a baby –
and we mark our days against its slow tick-tock.

A room is lit by moonbeams in a jar –
a sheen of navy-pearl like high midnight.
There's no red hint of dusk or dawn in there,
just rising thoughts of warning and delight.

I watched the moon once. It looked at me
and blinked, dropped its gaze in time
to stop me giving in to love or lunacy.
A light bulb moon will never wax or wane

so open the door. There are fire-flies outside.
While we've been talking, some were born and some died.

Today's Special

is the full English
served on the starkers damask
   of your matchless waitress –
me – salt-scrubbed and squeaky
   and balanced on the granite breakfast bar.
Golden clouds of scrambled are
   spooned between my pinkening tits.
It's self service. Pick
   from the parquet of rashers along my thighs,
the slices of pudding which petal my navel
   alternating black and white,
the figleaf triangle of toast,
   wholemeal, its butter curl
about to relax its constituent parts,
   sunshine and oil.
If you're still not full,
   the picnic's also in my repertoire:
sandwiches arranged in rows
   down my left side, up my right side,
bite-sized, ham or cheese
   set like a gambit in chess.
Once I laid out tea for two
   face down: split scone,
clotted cream, bramble jam
   on the lazy susan of my bum.
Every social situation
   comes off in the context of rules.
While punctilious insistence
   on the niceties of etiquette
is the mark of a snob, or a lack

of ease in company – diner,
a reminder, do not overfill your plate.
    Compliment your hostess.
It's rude to use your knife to point.
    This feast has hollowed the fridge.
We're down to the crumbs of the cake you made last week
    when you ran your finger round the bowl
and held it out. And your breakfast's
    getting cold. So come on now. Dig in.

Poem To Be Read on One Breath: Red

to convince a man confused by my meaningless millionaire's postcode that I am no raging materialist I tell him that everything I ever want I write hence this description of a pug with suede covered muffin top neck folds, a red leather leash and a seat by my side on all but the longest train journeys and though the man says he loves me on what is only the second ever visit to the flat I let him down shortly after very gently with a no kiss email

Poppet

Since you came apart from me
I've made a doll. I willed your offcut twin
from shadow-flat pieces of pinstripe and chamois,
held it up to its knees in my cool hand,
and filled it with a meal of pulses.
Relax, I whispered to the laws of physics,
then watched a doll soul knit itself together,
a pair of your cuff buttons flicker and blink.

He sits where the evening sun hits, or I prop him
up against the radio for the treble flutter.
He hangs like a charm off my necklace,
or I lay him down with hot water bottles
and a wound-up alarm clock in his bed,
like you would a weaning puppy.
Heat and ticking heartbeats all the time
since you came apart from me.

Like a Monkey Fighting a Lizard, Endlessly

'Our brain can be separated into three sections – our lizard brain, our monkey brain, and our human brain'

DR HEIDI HANNA

If you've just joined us, you're tuned
   to a battle royal, primate v reptile,
a bout that proves impossible to call.
   You've missed The Monkey – barely out
of its black silk robe – lamp and floor
   The Lizard with a set piece:
a one-two-three of feinting paws
   blocking the eyes and ears, guard up
on the gum-shield grin; and The Lizard
   charged by the spotlight, countering
with its heat ray eyeballs and bitter skin.
   Oh, now The Monkey's flinging words
like raining blows: blam,
   prehensile's made the canvas drum
and thwack, *opposability*'s a move
   that has The Lizard pinned. See that?
With no more thought than we would give
   to swapping a pair of shoes, it's slipped
itself out of its tail, sauntered to its corner,
   new tail sprouting like a watered bean
and The Monkey is stuck with a puzzle, a pawful
   of squirm. On and on they tussle,
this Airfix Godzilla and the Steiff King Kong
   but that bass ping from the struck bell
brings this gorgeous creature into the ring,
   wearing golden trunks which seem

still hot and liquid from the smelt,
    holding a numbered card to the crowds –
numbers they can't make out in the small print
    needed for all those figures to fit.
Look at the crowds, drawn to the fight
    in a headlock of cheers and groans,
sucked back yawns and bristling chins.
    Somebody's sneaking a look at the clock
but while these rivals, at the height of their game,
    at the top of the bill, are still on their stools
resetting for another round,
    it isn't time for home. Poor souls.

Monkey Puzzle

Outside every semi that I've owned
they've stood – incumbents of the front lawns,
holding their wintergreen limbs against the sky,
all silhouette. All snakes and elbows. Hand
on their bark, you will not feel the pulse of sap –
just the force of setting amber, their cold blood.

Beseech them pink and white to bloom
with candle flowers, to let their cherries drop
or launch their helicopter seeds into the air:
they won't. Their dapple filters never worked.
Through their angled branches, light falls
in broken tiles. I think of them as bishops.

Poem To Be Read on One Breath: Gold

to live like this in London is to look for something hundreds
of miles and dozens of years away so when the short, round,
old Italian man who is always in the café on my way to work
and who speaks only slightly more English than I speak Italian
which is none but has somehow still managed to tell me that
his wife has died and his wife is now his slow, gold, old Rolls
Royce points to his tomatoey breakfast or the sun and grins I
always grin back

Script for a Lecture on the English Rabbit for a W.I. eg

Right then, welcome. Phones off? Thank you. Please
don't rustle or heckle or cough. Lovely. Now,

breed standards for the English Rabbit,
the standards that rabbit show judges want to see,
are based on a painting of a rabbit, dreamt up
then realised by one Robert Wippell in 1838.

Robert painted *Rabbit as a Checklist*, making
white pelts a key target, adding contrast ears
in one of only blue, black, grey, tortoiseshell
or chocolate. Eye rings. A stripe along the spine
like herringbone. Flank marks, a beauty spot
and finally, the 'smut': the butterfly patch on the nose
as if a sooty Painted Lady perched there,
shook its dark into the fur and disappeared.

The rabbit matching this description, the perfect
spit, has never yet been bred, but burrowed
through my garden is a warren for a colony
of also-rans: rabbits with domino
white spots, rabbits born panda and zebra,
chess-board and Friesian, self-coloured bucks
like jars of paintbrush water, does in shades
of peach, blonde and duck egg whose litters
are swatches of postbox, JCB and serge.
There's one who rocks a hi-vis neon bobtail,
one who glows when the sun goes down and one
transparent, bold as glass. I'm sorry Robert, ladies,
and members of the National English Rabbit Club
but this month-old kit, her fur a rule book
in black or blue and white is not curled in my palm
like she's tucked in a nest, and does not exist.

Press Play

Load too much credit in the jukebox
    and every single ever written
        starts to play at once.

Vocals and bass lines,
    choruses and middle eights,
        session brass, children's choirs, sitars

swept up in a high tide of soundwaves
    lining up and clicking home
        and wiping themselves out.

The composite hit
    is a white wall of sound.
        Decibels unreadable as silence.

II

Replay and overlay us the last time
    with every time that's gone before.
        You, me, and. You, me, or.

Touch is papered over touch
    like a ricked joint rubbed numb,
        or gooseflesh on sunburn.

Like a stack of transparencies
    held to the light, such
        chaotic couplings –

a pinned or stretching limb
    in every second of a circle, some
        bomb blast or star burst. Some chrysanthemum.

III

With the white noise on repeat,
    attune yourself till every cell
        buzzes like a snare drum

and pick them out:
    that run of double claps,
        Minnie's head-notes, shattering.

A low sliding scale of Tom,
    and the song that holds its nerve
        on the fadeout rainstorm.

Welcome to Chinatown

I've been out, and everywhere I went I saw
the same albino gorilla. Blown-rose eyes,
old newsprint fur, star of the zoo

and the zoo shop, his features papped onto T-shirts
and action figures. White silverbacks or
crocodiles or bears: their skin

so stark and shadowless, they blush, their keepers swear.
Tutankhamun's everywhere as well.
If not the Boy King's jackpot mask

then his grave goods: the yoyos and the Haribo
which scattered when his layers were unwrapped.
Prizes all round when the music stopped.

I've picked the Water Lily from every gallery,
seen the gargoyle moon from every church.
Each dock-to-trickle river trip

with multilingual travel guides
takes me further from my first airport,
my first passport whose pages were once white; and drops me only

in the smallest hamlet in the county, at a pub with Domesday stars
where a shelf above the till in the back bar
holds a solar powered plastic

lucky fortune cat, paw at an angle for constantly
beckoning wealth. Welcome to Chinatown.
Stand here for the photograph.

Self Portrait with 40 Foot of Banquet Roll

The caterer's perfected the technique
of kick-pleats in the paper tablecloths,
and half an hour before the party starts,
the whole hall is quietly rustling. Each place
has a paper plate and a two-ply serviette
sharply finessed to one of three shapes:
lily follows mitre follows swan
round and round the rectangular trestles.
Where there might be children, there are crayons
and printed placemats for them to colour in.
Everyone will have a pack of streamers.
By the swinging kitchen door, there's one
or two already thrown. The caterer
has still to lay each setting with a cracker
pondering its own gunpowder heart,
a wax paper beaker, and one from a stack
of tiny cardboard tents, each hallmarked
with gold foil decals and a calligraphic name.

Three Poems
for Margaret
Fountaine

By the black arrow on the *You Are Here* board
you shall know your place. There's not a chance
it zips about the map like an insect
when *You're Not*, buzzing your steps
down Anchor Street, up Gaol Hill and through
Labour-in-Vain Yard, it's fixed:

[32]

a grid reference, a time stamp between
the square inch of green denoting playing field
and the pink patch that means church
on the map where every river and road
has been explored and named. It's fixed like a moth
that scans horizons from its pin.

Walls built of coins, a roof tiled with credit cards.
Dreamt-of colour; each coat of paint a shade closer.
Indoor air holding the charge of each dust-up
and reconciliation – I thought these in combination

made a house a home. But under the bed in a hotel room
high above the Danube, my lost watch still glows.
Fish I fed crumbs from a boat in the Aegean
fed fish which go on feeding fish; and flattened grass

in Central Park marks the spot I sat and ate
the minutes from an apple. Small and smaller deeds
in a widening world cut me a bunch of keys
I'll never lose – they'll let me in again, should I return.

Hem-deep, I love the gentle hustle of this brook,
how each step rocks and resettles the pebble bed,
cooling me down and calling me clean.
Where the water touches me, welcome home.

A girl points, and a swallowtail lands on her finger –
its body a blink, its wingtips spilling tiny swirls
that stir up the air above her till a breeze unknots and swells,
and thermals mass in a rabble of gale force and hailstones,

flash floods and lightning bolts, set to hit
the seaboard of a distant continent.
But she looks for the kink in the jet stream that turns a storm,
and forecasts sun. Failing that, a fall of clear rain.

Party, 1 a.m.

The playlist's last song.
  It's the first kiss tune
of half the steady, split
  or figment couples
in the room.

  Drink, that on dilution
turns to rainclouds
  in the glass,
is all the drink that's left.
  Everything soft has gone.

One guest has lost
  a black silk clutch
with a ruffle rose sewn on
  and till it's found
she can't get home.

  Of all the tealights
lit and set down
  in china saucers, one
is still awake.
  Its blown flame

dithers and jumps
  as if in response
to a trick question.
  Jason, mister: should we
set off or go on?

Koko the Signing Gorilla Tells Us About Her Day

fat orange fruit
fat orange fruit up
bird up
Koko sleep
Koko fake sleep
bird bird up
Koko up

Koko toothbrush lip lip
toothbrush nose
toothbrush stomach
polite toilet
sorry

Koko eat apple
eat orange
eat sandwich
good good
drink red devil candy drink

Koko browse
Koko stamp
Koko fine
Koko browse
Koko stamp
Koko fine

Koko ask
baby
pink baby

polite
rotten shame
love light

light old
fat orange fruit old
Koko ask sleep
want sleep
unattention
fake unattention

The Boast

As a girl, I won badges for this skill:
  campfires lit with pages of *The Wilts & Glos*,
a ration of leaf-mould and a single match.
  A firelighter is a little cube of poison fudge.
Even now, from a pile of pigeon moult,
  a rasping Zippo and a damp receipt,
I can spark it up. I'll kindle you a blaze
  that frees the sun-flare trapped inside a pine's
heart-wood: a snapping, spitting fire
  that draws up a chimney like a fervent prayer,
a fire that stirs a room's whole air
  to heat haze, that shows itself in miniature
in glass and metal, skin and porcelain, a fire
  that warms you through but scorches in a second
any letter you may choose to burn.
  In the morning, when you think the hearth is dead,
I'll find the dull red sweeties in the ash
  and, with a twist of paper handkerchief
and whispered streams of coaxing spells,
  will breed a bed of yellow crocus flames.
Yellow dancing girls. Orange generals
  who will follow any orders that I make.
When we've charred our way through every forest,
  torched our chopped up chairs and kicked in doors;
when all that's left to warm up in the embers
  is crab-apples and stones, you may call me on this boast.

Poem to be Read on One Breath: Emerald

you will occasionally bump into on your way to get the Saturday *Guardian*, some Maltesers and a pint of milk, a young woman with undone hair and a face bare of everything but coat pocket Lypsyl, wearing taxi shoes and a sequinned dress designed for the flat white light of morning the way an emerald tree frog is camouflaged on a beach and you know that she's just another girl making the Walk of Shame though that is not what shame feels like to you, not at all

Love Poem, with Artemia nyos

On page six of the giftware catalogue
there are Sea Monkeys: mail order sachets
of desiccated shrimp, their lives on pause
till you tick the tank you want – the Basic Model
or the Deep Sea Castle – and you fill it up, like
making instant noodles or orange squash.
The water brings them back to life. Little
dots of grit sprout legs and eyes. Look
through the tank wall's built-in lens to see.
There are few accessories to buy –
no wheels or mirror bells, no squeaky bones
or Good Boy chocolate drops – but how at night
their simple forms might sparkle in the play
of the three-colour torch on page eight.

As they pulled you out of the oxygen tent / you asked for the latest party

Of all our friends, he's the one
most serious about the art of fancy dress.
Every cupboard in his flat is stuffed
with bags of outfits and face-paint,
feathered half-masks and costume diamonds.
Once, before a Monochrome Ball,
we fed him penny liquorice chews
to change the red bell of his mouth to black;
and if the dress code is drag, our tallest girl
lends him her highest heels and he'll stand
all night at an angle slightly off from true
with the muscles bunching in his back
and fire in the arches of his feet.
Tonight, the theme is Saints and Sinners.
Wearing only dark high-waisted trousers,
he is topless and his skin we say
is markedly pale as that of a Charolais calf.
Ask him who he is. He's Sebastian,
a half an hour before the arrows hit.
In eight places, we can see his heart beat.

Parrot Spotter

So, the oaks and the hazels are dripping wet.
That doesn't make this the rainforest.

Parrots, in their car horn colours
working their fascinator tails

their secateur beaks
and dinned-in roller skating skills,

are not vaulting through the canopy
effing and blinding their pirate eloquence.

We've come here in what will be the last
of your four new red Fiestas.

Heat leaves the bonnet as the engine rests.
Trees undo their rings another notch.

That flare of brick and bluebell through the leaves,
that one sharp cry – it might have been a jay.

There are Sixty-two Pieces of Lego for Every Person on the Planet

I do not have sixty-two pieces of Lego.
Neither do my mum, my brother
    nor his wife; nor my boss,
    my best friend in Devon,
my best friend in London,
my right-hand next-door neighbour,
    nor my left-hand next-door neighbour
    and the man I met once in a pub in Brixton
did not have, as far as I remember,
sixty-two pieces of Lego either –
    so one of you has skewed the maths
    and must have in your stash
six hundred and twenty
pieces of Lego to yourself, at least.
    Let's not make this
    some cack-handed critique
of twenty first century capitalism
pitting those who've bought and built and own
    the three thousand, eight hundred and three brick
    Star Wars Lego Death Star
with movie-authentic environments
including the Superlaser control room
    the Emperor's throne room,
    droid maintenance room,
detention block, trash compactor,
and much more against those
    without a single Lego person
    to their name, not one
with those rigid little legs
and hinging waists

so that though they cannot kick
   they can bow, most deeply, down.
Let us rather
praise the canny statistician
   who organised the counting station
   at the Lego factory gates,
with a clicker in each hand
to monitor the global births
   and death rates on the right
   and with the left, the leaving lorry-loads
of inch-high window frames and corner bricks.
conical trees and 3 by 2s.
   Let us spend a minute
   give or take two seconds,
building something colourful for her or him
imagining our rightful allocation
   into wide and oblong cars
   with eight ridiculous sets of wheels,
or elaborate rifles with buttressed barrels,
or poky ticket kiosks
   with mosaic brickwork
   with huge red sloping roofs.
Fill a large green rigid baseboard
with red and white and yellow blooms
   on plastic triplet stems.
   Five dozen and one of them.

Poem to be Read on One Breath: Rose

each time I go to Wagamama and most times it's the branch beneath the Royal Festival Hall I have *amai udon* and because the prawns though moreish and repellent in equal part for being at the same time rose and worm invariably total the number the recipe spreadsheet on the back of the kitchen door dictates, the syntax of my poems is, for the most part, perfect

If You Do That, I Am Forced To Do This

Though you won't know it
I'm making meringues,

the glass cooker door screening
a film I've seen already.

Angry white kittens
with their fur on end.

to be shone on his body

(*title sequence to a film*)

hope in rose-gold twists at the spot
    where the spirit   where the thought is

honey-coloured appetite cartwheeling
    where the parting   where the want is

saffron-dipped faith on its toes on his skin
    where the fret   where the bite is

pilot-light fears butterfly   blue
    where the heat   where the heart is

light gold-leaf delight somersaults
    where the nightmare   where the art is

It's Not The Years, Honey, It's the Mileage

There are places where it doesn't hurt:
elbow, forehead, eyelid, lips.
If you won't ask me, I'll make you ask me –
a kiss felt in a million mouths.

Elbow, forehead, eyelid, lips.
One kiss used, then lost, then sold to a museum,
a kiss felt in a million mouths,
a story with sequels and sub-text.

One kiss used, then lost, then sold to a museum.
I'm not the first girl to have travelled with pirates
(a story with sequels and sub-text).
Sometimes we all go out in a borrowed dress.

I'm not the first girl to have travelled with pirates.
Scrapes and grazes, bullet nicks.
Sometimes we all go out in a borrowed dress,
a lovely moon-rock coloured dress.

Scrapes and grazes, bullet nicks.
If you won't ask me, I'll make you ask me.
A lovely moon-rock coloured dress.
There are places where it doesn't hurt.

Poem in Which God at 1% is Acknowledged

All year, the pile of red bills grows.
The final demands and the urgent requests
to settle this account are rammed in drawers
and shoved behind the clock
till somewhere on the circuit
which links sub-station to socket
a coupling snaps
and the dark is switched back on.
And it's nothing but relief:
darkness restored and rinsed of light
like white paint washed
from a black cat.
Without the blare of the chandelier,
the spotlight, the striplight or the LED
the quiet cue of the sunshine's bowing out is caught.
Without shadows, without dusk or doubt
there is no prompt to clarify the flicker
of a secret story seen from the side of your eye,
no need to ask what happens next
and then what happens after that.
This is the answer, mark it with a tick:
the ghost-green hands of a luminous watch
left on a bedside table –
eleven-o-five and all's well.
In the dark we recognise the blue half moon
at the base of a candle's almond flame,
and catch sight of the young aunt
who's writing her niece's name in air

with the cherry end of her glowing cigarette,
who blows a smoky kiss
and is off into the night.

Poem to be Read on One Breath: Blue

I am bathing my toddler nephew and doing so cautiously as there are so many ways to shopsoil someone else's child in a setting such as this such as scalding or drowning or man o' war attack but still we are having a useful chat about plastic seafood tub toys during which I say *octopus* and he says *doctoper* and I say *octopus* and he says *octoper* and I say *octopus* and he says *octopus* and I see the blue flash flash as the relevant neurone wriggles its tentacles into place and locks them down forever

A Pebble Cairn

All I've ever taken is a stone
from every beach I've stood on:

    agate and flint,
    quartzite and slate.

All I've ever taken is a stone
from every beach I've stood on –

    a pebble cairn,
    a coast for each room.

All I've ever taken is a stone
from every beach I've stood on.

    To stand on a beach
    is to count the waves in.

All I've ever taken is a stone
from every beach I've stood on:

    marble sunset.
    Night swim in sandstone.

All I've ever taken is a stone
from every beach I've stood on –

when to return them
to the beaches they came from?

All I've ever taken is a stone
from every beach I've stood on.

Victoria Street Reel

A band strikes up. A bendy bus
gives us a tune on its grey accordion.
Taxis taking the corner chug
third gear, first gear, third gear bass
and the pelican crossing beeps up a rhythm.
On the pavement, two queues:
one for the night club, one for the night bus.
The passengers are cosy in their cloud-
and tarmac-coloured overcoats,
their sigh-coloured scarves. The club kids
have done it – gone out – dressed like *that*
in rowdy tans and magazine looks
all set to dip the backlit bottles at the bar
and mix their drinks their own sweet way.

When this bit of the night has played,
the bus queue and the club queue pull apart
to the left, the right, a slow jilt.
But if the last in line in each
should catch their partner's eye
and trip an accidental bow
then this is called *an honour*
and this is part of dancing.

The Preservation of Flowers

Between the cab firm and the chicken shop
the pavement cracked and a flower stall sprang up,
the city's special offer to the passer by.
It stocks every colour flower except grey,
twenty-four seven blossom, the odds on bees,
and a sign which says *You Can Smell The Flowers for Free.*
It checks the street. Those who used to hurry
are slowed, and sold on bouquets of *gorgeous* and *sorry.*
They pick the florist too. He's a bunch
of bluebell eyes and blooming sales pitch,
daisy grin and hip-slung money belt,
lily pollen brushed across his shirt.
Certain customers, he slips an extra rose
in the dozen; to certain customers he says
'Angel – if you want them to last a little bit longer
add a teaspoon of sugar to the water.'

Notes

32 Girls

A British Council commission on the theme of inter-generational dialogue, for posters on Brussels' underground system.

On Visiting A Church Built to the Same Dimensions as Noah's Ark

... which St Bartholomew's Church in Brighton supposedly is.

Bones

Written for a Monopoly-themed poetry night.

You Could Be Better Off Than You Are

A Southbank Centre commission, written for a performance during the Hayward Gallery's *Light Show* exhibition. Katie Paterson's 'Light bulb to Simulate Moonlight' consists of a single lightbulb, engineered to replicate moonlight, hanging in a small room. It also has a log book and a sufficient quantity of spare bulbs to provide a lifetime's supply. The title of the poem is a version of a line from 'Swinging on a Star', music by Jimmy Van Heusen, lyrics by Johnny Burke.

Script for a Lecture on the English Rabbit for a W.I.eg

More details about English Rabbit breed standards at www.national-english.moonfruit.com

Press Play

Minnie Riperton was famed for her high notes, Tom Waits is for his low ones.

Three Poems for Margaret Fountaine

A Writers' Centre Norwich commission. Margaret Fountaine, born in Norwich in 1862, lived the trammelled life of a Victorian vicar's daughter until a timely bequest allowed her the freedom to devote her life to butterfly collecting. She travelled all over the world in pursuit of them, becoming one of the foremost entomologists of her day. Her diaries – which record her adventurous love life in as much detail as her butterfly studies – are kept at Norwich Castle Museum.

The streets named in the first poem are all in Norwich. The countries referred to in the second poem (Hungary, Turkey and America) are some of the countries visited by both Margaret and me. Swallowtail butterflies are rare in Britain, but when they are found, it is only in the east of the country. 'Rabble' is a collective noun for butterflies.

Natascha Scott-Stokes' life of Margaret Fountaine, *Wild & Fearless* (Peter Owen, 2006) was most useful during the writing of the poems.

Koko the Signing Gorilla Tells Us About Her Day

More details about Koko here www.koko.org

The Boast

An Aldeburgh Lookout commission, written after staying overnight in the beach Lookout Tower, in February.

As they pulled you out of the oxygen tent / you asked for the latest party

Inspired by David Sims' photographic exhibition *Bowievirus* at the ICA. The title of the poem is a line from *Diamond Dogs*, music and lyrics by David Bowie.

There Are Sixty-two Pieces of Lego for Every Person on the Planet

... makes use of text from the Lego website.

It's Not The Years, Honey, It's The Mileage

Written for an Indiana Jones-themed poetry night to celebrate the 30th anniversary of *Raiders of the Lost Ark*.

Victoria Street Reel

In country dancing or square dancing, an honour is the bow or curtsy you give to your dancing partner.